I Unpacked My Grandmother's Trunk

A PICTURE BOOK GAME

by Susan Ramsay Hoguet

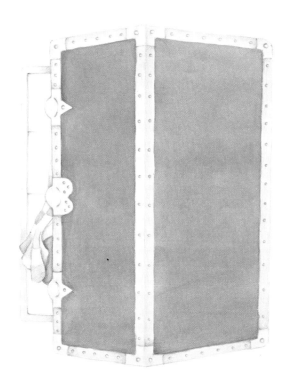

OXFORD UNIVERSITY PRESS

Copyright © 1983 by Susan Ramsay Hoguet

Oxford University Press, Walton Street, Oxford OX2 6DP

Oxford   New York   Toronto
Delhi   Bombay   Calcutta   Madras   Karachi
Petaling Jaya   Singapore   Hong Kong   Tokyo
Nairobi   Dar es Salaam   Cape Town
Melbourne   Auckland

and associated companies in
Beirut   Berlin   Ibadan   Nicosia

Oxford is a trade mark of Oxford University Press

First published in the USA 1983 by E. P. DUTTON, INC.
Reprinted 1985

Printed by Dai Nippon Printing Co., Ltd., Tokyo, Japan

Directions for playing
I Unpacked My Grandmother's Trunk

This game can be played with two or more players. It is an excellent car game.

The first player says, "I unpacked my grandmother's trunk, and out of it I took an acrobat" (or any other object beginning with *a*).

The second player says, "I unpacked my grandmother's trunk, and out of it I took an acrobat and a bear" (or any other object beginning with *b*).

The third player (or the first, if only two are playing) says, "I unpacked my grandmother's trunk, and out of it I took an acrobat, a bear, and a cloud" (or any other object beginning with *c*).

Each player in turn adds a new object for the appropriate letter of the alphabet after listing *all* the previously named objects. The first time a player forgets to mention a previously named object or mentions one in the wrong order, that player must drop out of the game. The last player still in the game is the winner.

If using this book for the game, players should first go through the book, then close it and play the game from memory.

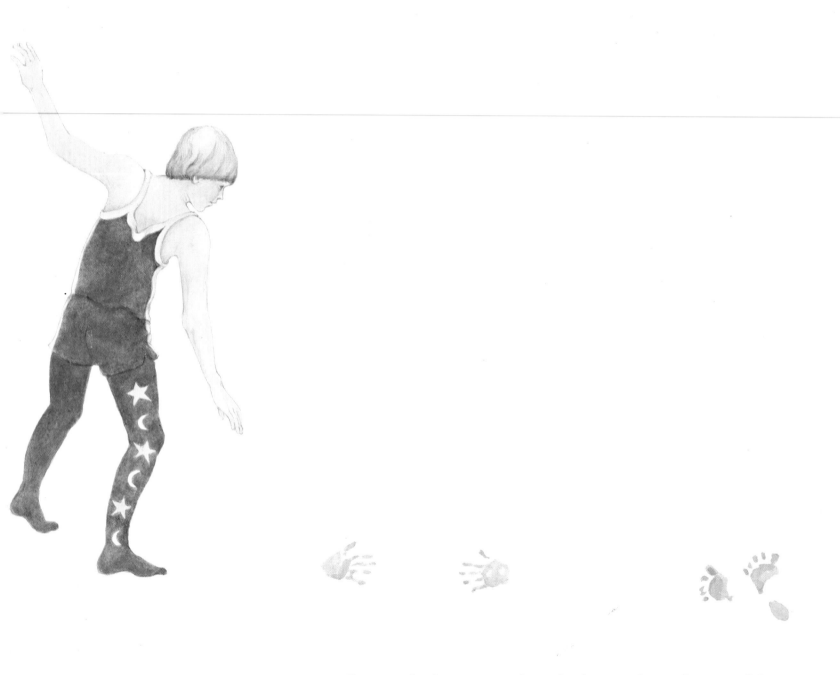

I unpacked my grandmother's trunk, and out of it
I took an acrobat.

an acrobat and a bear.

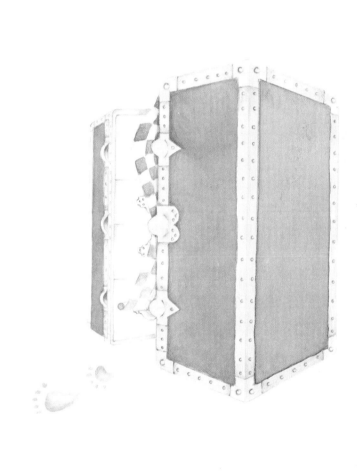

an acrobat, a bear, and a cloud.

an acrobat, a bear, a cloud, and a dinosaur.

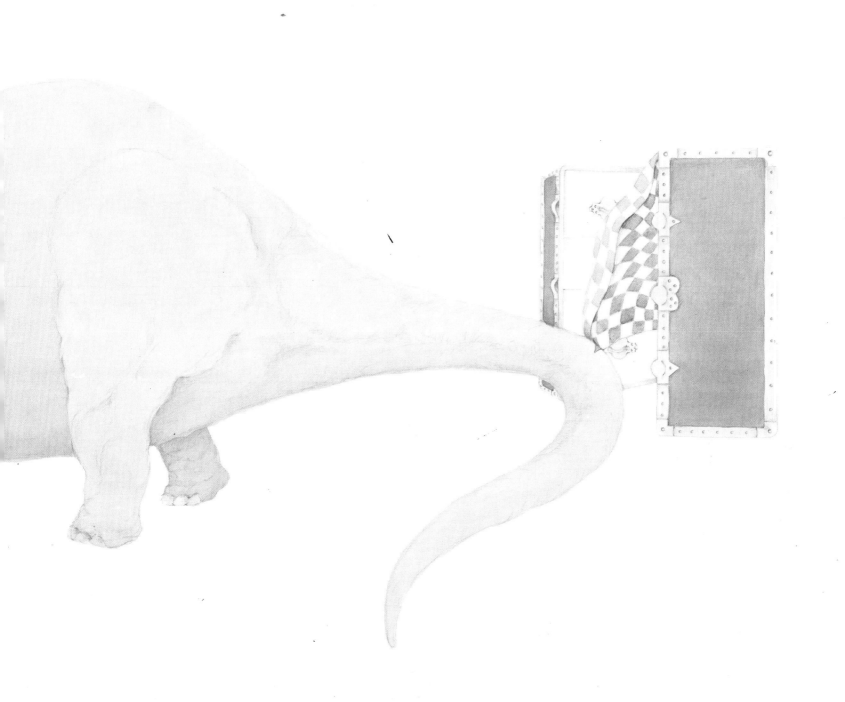

an acrobat, a bear, a cloud, a dinosaur, and an eagle.

an acrobat, a bear, a cloud, a dinosaur, an eagle,
and a fairy.

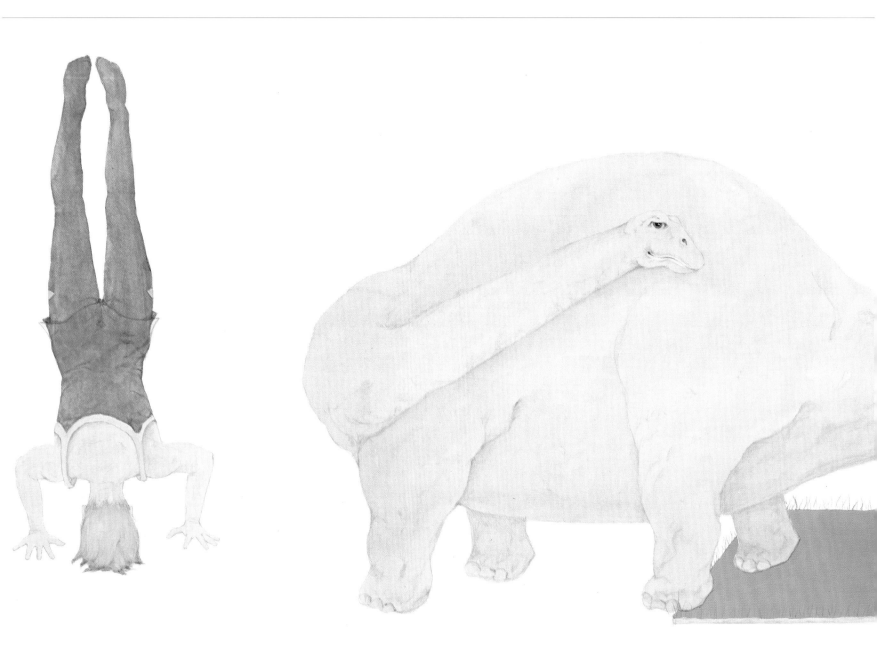

an acrobat, a bear, a cloud, a dinosaur, an eagle, a fairy, and some grass.

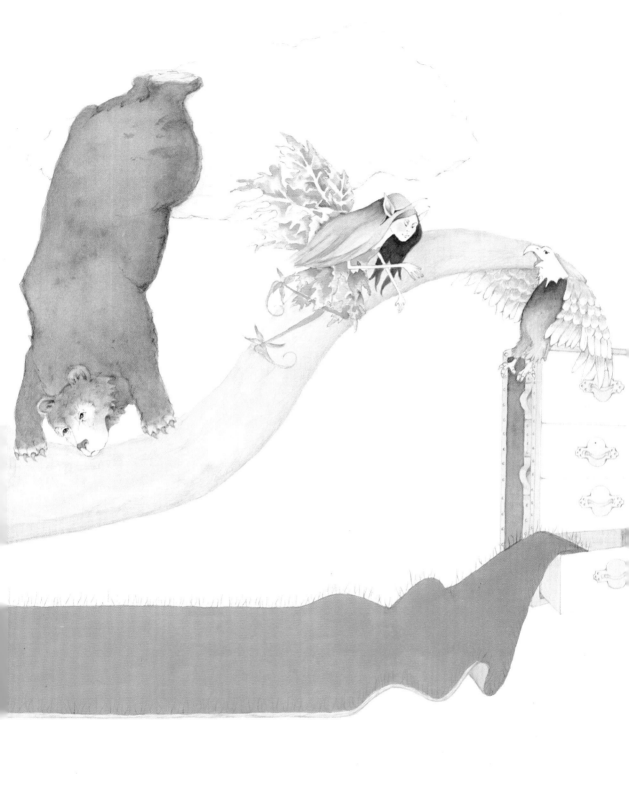

an acrobat, a bear, a cloud, a dinosaur, an eagle, a fairy, some grass, and a hat.

an acrobat, a bear, a cloud, a dinosaur, an eagle, a fairy, some grass, a hat, and an igloo.

an acrobat, a bear, a cloud, a dinosaur, an eagle, a fairy, some grass, a hat, an igloo, and a jungle.

an acrobat, a bear, a cloud, a dinosaur, an eagle, a fairy,
some grass, a hat, an igloo, a jungle, and a kangaroo.

an acrobat, a bear, a cloud, a dinosaur, an eagle, a fairy, some grass, a hat, an igloo, a jungle, a kangaroo, and a lamp.

an acrobat, a bear, a cloud, a dinosaur, an eagle, a fairy,
some grass, a hat, an igloo, a jungle, a kangaroo, a lamp,
and a mouse.

an acrobat, a bear, a cloud, a dinosaur, an eagle, a fairy, some grass, a hat, an igloo, a jungle, a kangaroo, a lamp, a mouse, and a nest.

an acrobat, a bear, a cloud, a dinosaur, an eagle, a fairy, some grass, a hat, an igloo, a jungle, a kangaroo, a lamp, a mouse, a nest, and an ostrich.

an acrobat, a bear, a cloud, a dinosaur, an eagle, a fairy, some grass, a hat, an igloo, a jungle, a kangaroo, a lamp, a mouse, a nest, an ostrich, and a pagoda.

an acrobat, a bear, a cloud, a dinosaur, an eagle, a fairy, some grass, a hat, an igloo, a jungle, a kangaroo, a lamp, a mouse, a nest, an ostrich, a pagoda, and a queen.

an acrobat, a bear, a cloud, a dinosaur, an eagle, a
fairy, some grass, a hat, an igloo, a jungle, a kangaroo,
a lamp, a mouse, a nest, an ostrich, a pagoda, a queen,

and a rocking chair.

an acrobat, a bear, a cloud, a dinosaur, an eagle, a
fairy, some grass, a hat, an igloo, a jungle, a kangaroo,
a lamp, a mouse, a nest, an ostrich, a pagoda, a queen,

a rocking chair, and a snowman.

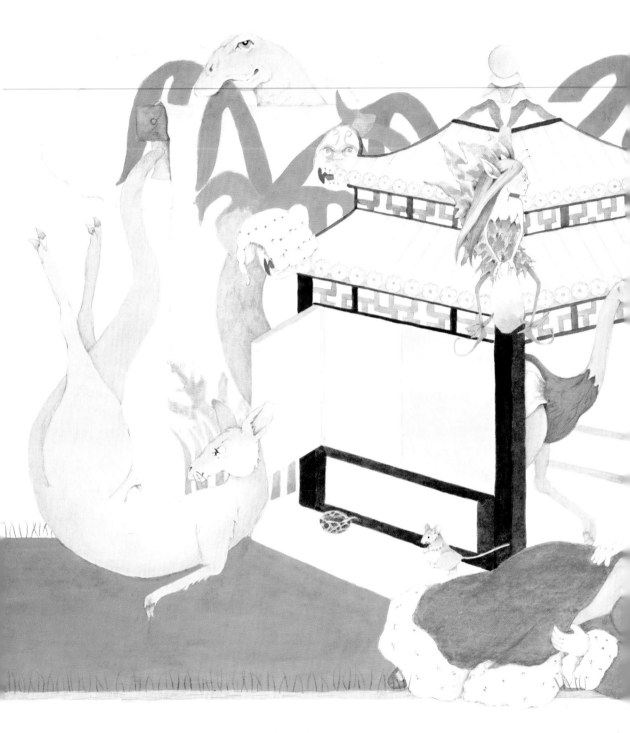

an acrobat, a bear, a cloud, a dinosaur, an eagle, a
fairy, some grass, a hat, an igloo, a jungle, a kangaroo,
a lamp, a mouse, a nest, an ostrich, a pagoda, a queen,

a rocking chair, a snowman, and a tiger.

an acrobat, a bear, a cloud, a dinosaur, an eagle, a
fairy, some grass, a hat, an igloo, a jungle, a kangaroo,
a lamp, a mouse, a nest, an ostrich, a pagoda, a queen,

a rocking chair, a snowman, a tiger, and an umbrella.

an acrobat, a bear, a cloud, a dinosaur, an eagle, a
fairy, some grass, a hat, an igloo, a jungle, a kangaroo,
a lamp, a mouse, a nest, an ostrich, a pagoda, a queen,

a rocking chair, a snowman, a tiger, an umbrella, and
a valentine.

an acrobat, a bear, a cloud, a dinosaur, an eagle, a
fairy, some grass, a hat, an igloo, a jungle, a kangaroo,
a lamp, a mouse, a nest, an ostrich, a pagoda, a queen,

a rocking chair, a snowman, a tiger, an umbrella, a valentine, and a windmill.

an acrobat, a bear, a cloud, a dinosaur, an eagle, a
fairy, some grass, a hat, an igloo, a jungle, a kangaroo,
a lamp, a mouse, a nest, an ostrich, a pagoda, a queen,

a rocking chair, a snowman, a tiger, an umbrella, a valentine, a windmill, and a xylophone.

an acrobat, a bear, a cloud, a dinosaur, an eagle, a
fairy, some grass, a hat, an igloo, a jungle, a kangaroo,
a lamp, a mouse, a nest, an ostrich, a pagoda, a queen,

a rocking chair, a snowman, a tiger, an umbrella, a valentine, a windmill, a xylophone, and a yo-yo.

an acrobat, a bear, a cloud, a dinosaur, an eagle, a
fairy, some grass, a hat, an igloo, a jungle, a kangaroo,
a lamp, a mouse, a nest, an ostrich, a pagoda, a queen,

a rocking chair, a snowman, a tiger, an umbrella, a
valentine, a windmill, a xylophone, a yo-yo, and a zebra.

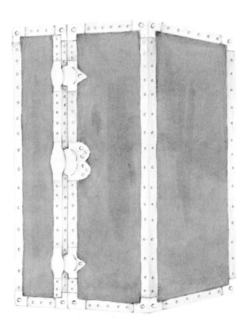